Darling Dinosaurs

Charted for Counted Thread, Embroidery and Applique

by Jean D. Crowther

Table of Contents

Acknowledgments

This book was made possible by the assistance of the following people:
Bessie Dean, who drew the original sketches,
Sharon Crowther and Sandi Rasband, who drafted the charts,
Tracy Price and Sharon Crowther, who stitched the models,
the typesetting, design and technical staff of Horizon Publishers,
and my husband, Duane, who kept us all moving towards the completion of the project.

Materials for the models were provided as follows:
Floss, from **DMC Corporation,** Elizabeth, NJ 07206-0413,
Country Linen Evenweave fabric, from **Regency Mills, Inc.,** East Newark, NY 07029,
Colored Aida cloth, **Charles Craft, Inc.,** Laurinburg, NC 28352,
Stitch 'n' Wash Sweatshirt and T-shirt, **Creative Keepsakes,** P.O. Box 7651, Monroe, LA 71203, and
All frames, **Wheatland Crafts, Inc.,** 834 Scuffleton Road, Simpsonville, SC 29681.

Sincere appreciation is extended to them all. I hope that you will enjoy using these charts and your imagination to create your own "Darling Dinosaurs!"

Jean Crowther

First Printing, June 1988

Printing: 1 2 3 4 5 6 7 8 9 10

ISBN: 0-88290-324-1

Horizon Publishers' Catalog and Order Number: 2775

Horizon Publishers
& Distributors, Incorporated
50 South 500 West P.O. Box 490
Bountiful, Utah 84010-0490

www.horizonpublishers.biz

DMC®

Applique Suggestions

Sharon's purple sweatshirt is appliqued with a lilac calico Brontosaurus. Bethany is wearing a light blue "Stitch 'n' Wash" sweatshirt. The Styracosaurus is stitched with a burgundy backstitch.

Sharon's deep red apron is decorated with a teal blue pin dot appliqued Tyronosaurus Rex.

Instructions

For Your Information: The dinosaurs ("terrible lizards") are an exciting part of the earth's history and appeal to the imagination of all age levels. Some species were the largest land animals that ever lived, but others were smaller than rabbits. Some dinosaurs swam in the oceans of their day, others had wings and could fly. Scientists accept them as the predecessors of both our reptiles and birds of today since all dinosaur hip bones can be classified as those two types.

They first appeared on the earth about 200 million years ago and inhabited it for about 70 million years during the Mesozoic era. At that time some unknown catastrophe killed them all. Until 1802, no one knew of their existance. A series of fossil discoveries during the next fifty years began the study of the creatures. Since only fossils remain, there is much information that scientists guess at and even disagree upon. The majority of the fossils have been bones and teeth, although some eggs and fossils of skin and other external features have been found. As other discoveries are made and studied, more will be added to our knowledge of these great creatures. In this book, a brief paragraph is included on each page with information about that specific specie of dinosaur. Names have been given to personalize the creatures.

Basic Cross-Stitch—Always be sure that your stitches cross in the same direction for a uniform appearance. If the bottom diagonal slants from the lower left hole to the upper right, all bottom diagonals in the piece should be worked in that same direction. (See Figure 1.)

Half Stitch—In some areas, the graph will show the symbol in only one corner of the square. To create this half stitch, work from the corner hole into the center of the square, placing the needle between the threads. Complete the stitch with a full diagonal in the color being used or complete it as part of the backstitch outline as indicated. (See Figure 2.)

Backstitch Outline—This stitch provides linear detail. Bring the needle up in the first hole indicated by the pattern. Place the needle down in the hole behind the initial stitch. Continue working one stitch-length back on top of the fabric, and two stitches forward beneath the fabric, to form a solid line. (See Figure 3.)

"Over-Two" and "Over-Three" Backstitch—To create a gentler line for the outlines, two stitches have been created. The terms "over-two" and "over-three" refer to the distance a single backstitch will travel over squares vertically or horizontally. (See Figure 4.)

When working the shadings, the area between the last complete stitched square and the line which will later be backstitched will need to be filled in with floss as designated. True half-stitches would be the wrong angle needed to cover these areas. Therefore, it is necessary to make short-angled stitches to fill in the area to be covered.

To fill in the area of an "over-two" stitch, begin at the corner hole of the narrowest part of the area and make a very shallow-angled half-stitch. The wider part of the area will need a steeper-angled half-stitch (perhaps with even the half-stitch crossed to completely fill in the area). (See Figure 5.) Leave the remaining stitches uncrossed. The "over-three" backstitch area will be filled in the same manner. (See Figure 6.) The backstitch color will later serve as the crossing stitch for the "over-two" and "over-three" areas. (See Figure 7.)

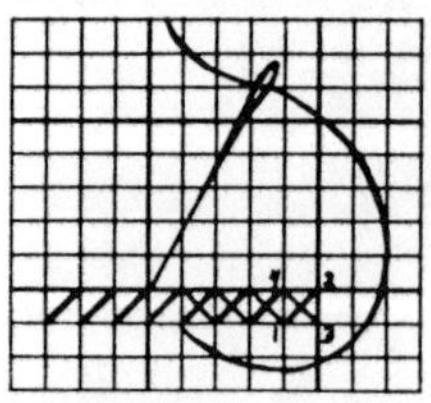

Fig. 1
Basic Cross-Stitch

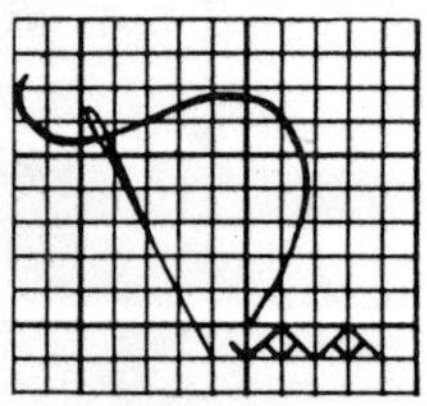

Fig. 2
Half Stitch

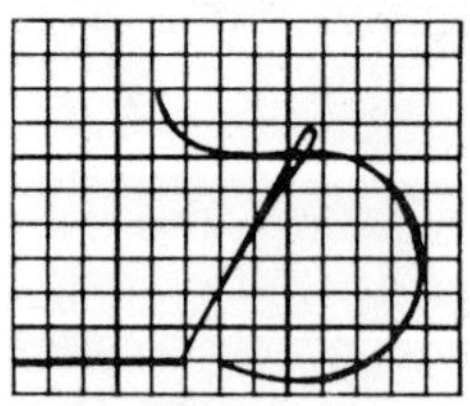

Fig. 3
Backstitch Outline

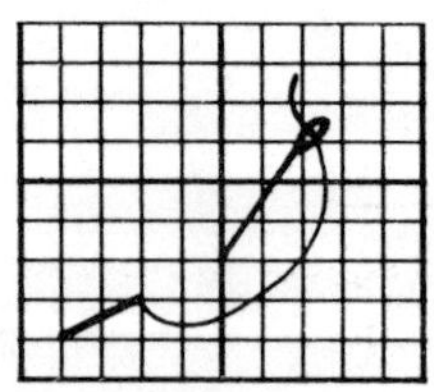

Fig. 4
Over-Two Backstitch

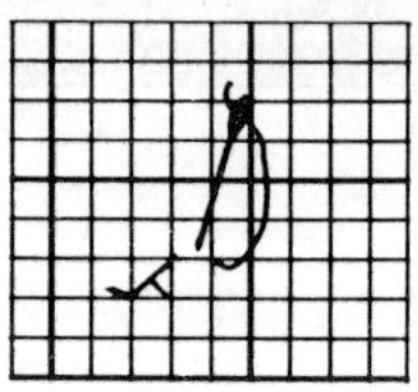

Fig. 5
Over-Two Fill-In Stitch

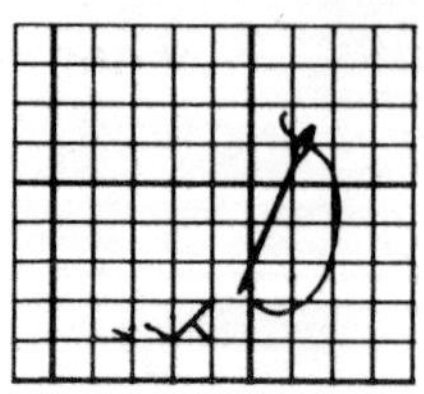

Fig. 6
Over-Three Fill-In Stitch

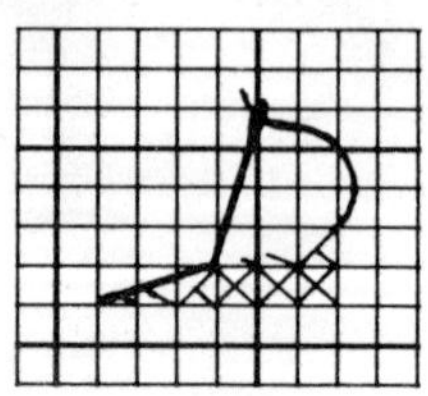

Fig. 7
Over-Three Backstitch & Fill-In Stitch

Stitchery Options. Several choices are available for the stitcher to use with these charts. Page 6 lists twenty-two color combinations. They are listed with four compatible shades from the darkest to the lightest. The number of strands of floss used is the individual choice of each stitcher and depends on the gauge of the material used. It is recommended that a hoop be used to keep the tensions of the floss even. Design sizes are given on each page for assistance in planning the finished product.

1. When solid stitching is desired, work the design with all four shades described on the color chart page.
2. When the outline and shading only is planned, either the second or third colors will be omitted.
3. The designs may be stitched as a single-color backstitch outline only in at least three ways:
   A. On even-weave material.
   B. On any material or article of clothing using waste canvas or washout graphs.
   C. Any material tracing outline with a transfer pencil with embroidery stitches.
4. The design may be traced and used as the outline for a material applique by following the steps outlined below:
   A. A product is now available which will make any material into an iron-on applique. One trade name is *Pellon Wonder-Under™ Transfer Web.*
   B. The design can be traced directly from this book onto the paper backing of this product. Remember this will reverse the design of the final applique. If the stitcher wishes the dinosaur to face the same direction as in the book, an intermediate reversed drawing should be made before tracing the design onto the paper backing.
   C. Following the manufacturer's directions, iron the rough side of the Transfer Web onto the wrong side of the material. Cut out the design and the material, then fuse it into place.
   D. The details inside the figure can be drawn onto the applique before ironing it on with a regular pencil or a disappearing ink product.
   E. Using a satin stitch of desired length, machine embroider around the outside of the applique. Add the details when stitching the applique down, probably using a narrower width than is used for the outside stitching. Placing the material carefully into a large hoop without stretching it might make this final stitching easier to do without buckling the applique or backing material.

Alphabet: This alphabet is provided to personalize the designs with the name of the dinosaur or other names.

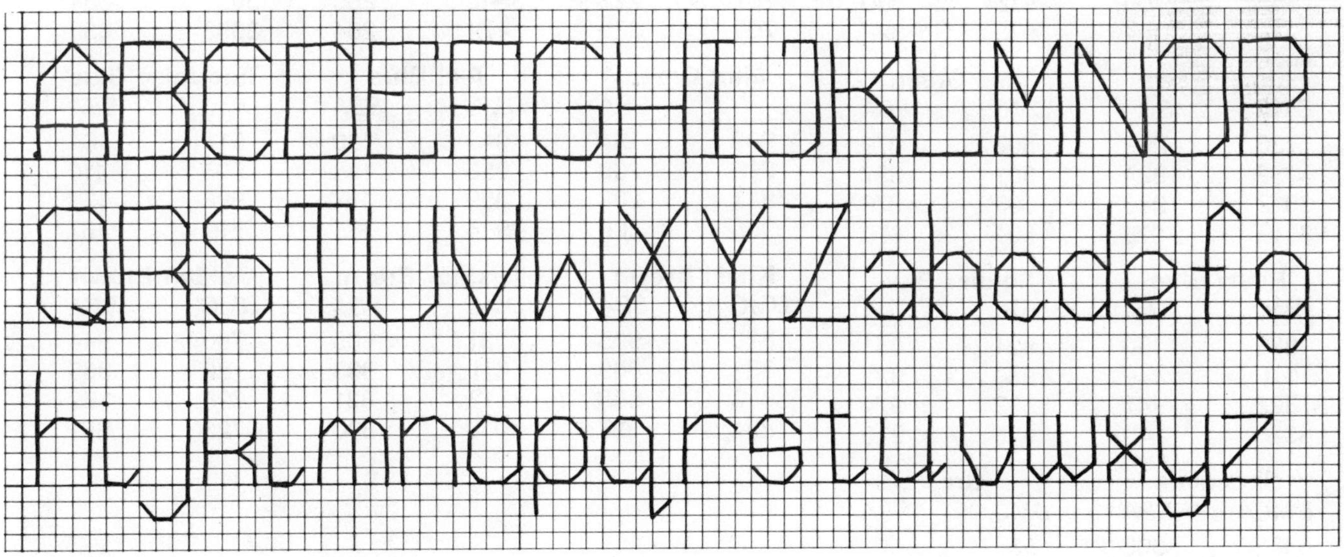

Color Chart

The following twenty-two color combinations have been chosen. Four compatible colors are listed in order from the darkest shade to the lightest. They can be used as follows:

1. When a solidly stitched figure is desired, the first (or darkest) color should be used for the backstitch outline (—). The second color is suggested for the dark shading (⁄), the third for the body of the figure (empty square within the design), and the last color for the light shading (•).
2. If the figure is to be worked with backstitch outline and shadings only, either the second or third color should be omitted. This is very attractive when worked on colored Aida cloth.
3. If the figure is backstitch-outlined only, the darkest shade will be best on light material, the lightest on dark-colored material.
4. The eyes may be worked with an outline only or with the pupils filled in (probably using the same color as the backstitch floss), or the whites can be filled in with white or cream. The claws, teeth, and/or horns may also be filled in with white or cream as desired.

The floss shades are given in either DMC or Susan Bates Anchor. However, the brands are not interchangeable within the specific color combination.

Dark Red

DMC	*SBA*
814	22
816	20
304	19
321	35

Bright Red

DMC	*SBA*
817	44
666	47
3705	46
3708	9

Fuchsia

DMC	*SBA*
600	89
602	88
604	87
605	85

Pink

DMC	*SBA*
326	29
335	27
3326	25
818	23

Salmon

DMC	*SBA*
817	20
350	13
3706	10
3708	8

Orchid

DMC	*SBA*
550	102
552	107
554	105
211	104

Orange

DMC	*SBA*
721	335
970	333
972	330
973	328

Kelly Green

DMC	*SBA*
890	923
699	229
701	227
703	225

Avocado Green

DMC	*SBA*
895	269
3346	267
3348	265
472	264

Olive Green

DMC	*SBA*
934	869
936	856
3051	854
3053	853

Lime Green

DMC	*SBA*
730	269
732	924
3012	280
3013	278

Sea Green

DMC	*SBA*
500	879
501	897
503	876
504	875

Mint Green

DMC	*SBA*
909	211
911	209
913	208
955	206

Teal Blue

DMC	*SBA*
943	189
958	188
959	187
964	185

Turquoise Blue

DMC	*SBA*
517	164
995	410
996	433
519	167

Royal Blue

DMC	*SBA*
823	150
311	149
322	147
3325	145

Soldier Blue

DMC	*SBA*
924	851
930	922
932	921
928	920

Khaki Brown

DMC	*SBA*
829	905
831	889
833	888
834	887

Leather Brown

DMC	*SBA*
3031	905
611	903
612	831
3033	830

Golden Brown

DMC	*SBA*
780	944
782	365
725	362
726	361

Chocolate

DMC	*SBA*
3371	360
801	359
434	936
436	379

Gray

DMC	*SBA*
535	401
317	400
318	399
762	397

Brenda Brontosaurus

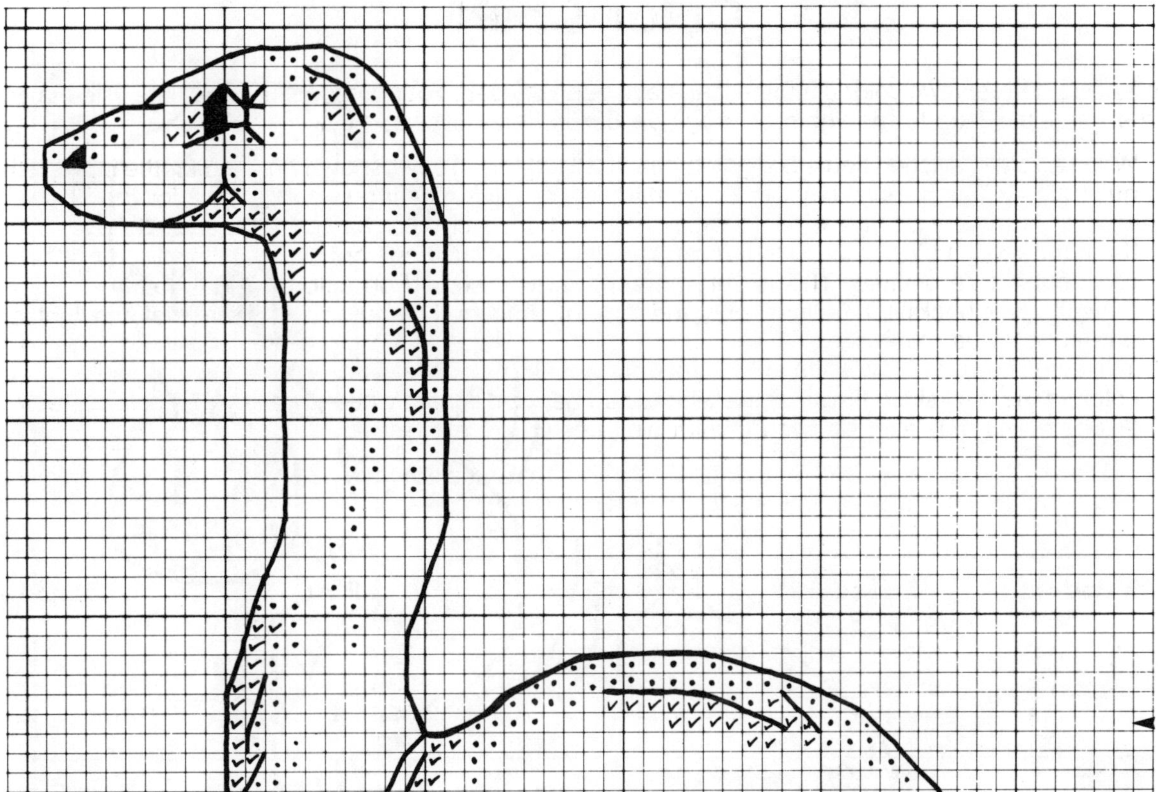

The model is stitched in the bright red color combination on white 14-count Aida cloth. It is mounted in Wheatland Crafts' 5" x 6" Thin Line frame. **Design size: 51 x 68**

Brontosaurus (bron-toe-SAWR-us) The name means "thunder lizard." She was a plant eater and lived in swampy areas where the water could help support her large body and partially protect her from her enemies. Although she walked on four feet and used her strong tail for defense, there is evidence that she could also rise up on her hind legs to reach leaves of tall trees. She is the best known of all the dinosaurs, but there have been two larger similar species found. She was about 60 feet long and weighed about 35 tons.

Anthony Anatosaurus

The model is stitched in the avocado color combination on green 14-count Aida cloth. It is mounted in Wheatland Crafts' 5" x 6" Thin Line frame.

Design size: 51 x 68

Anatosaurus (uh-nat-o-SAWR-us) The name means "duck lizard." He had a large mouth with over 2,000 rough teeth in it. It is believed that he ate reedy plants and usually walked upright on his three-toed back feet. His rough pebbly skin and evidence that his toes might have been webbed have been found. He probably lived near water and might have been able to swim. His size is uncertain.

Tyler Tyrannosaurus Rex

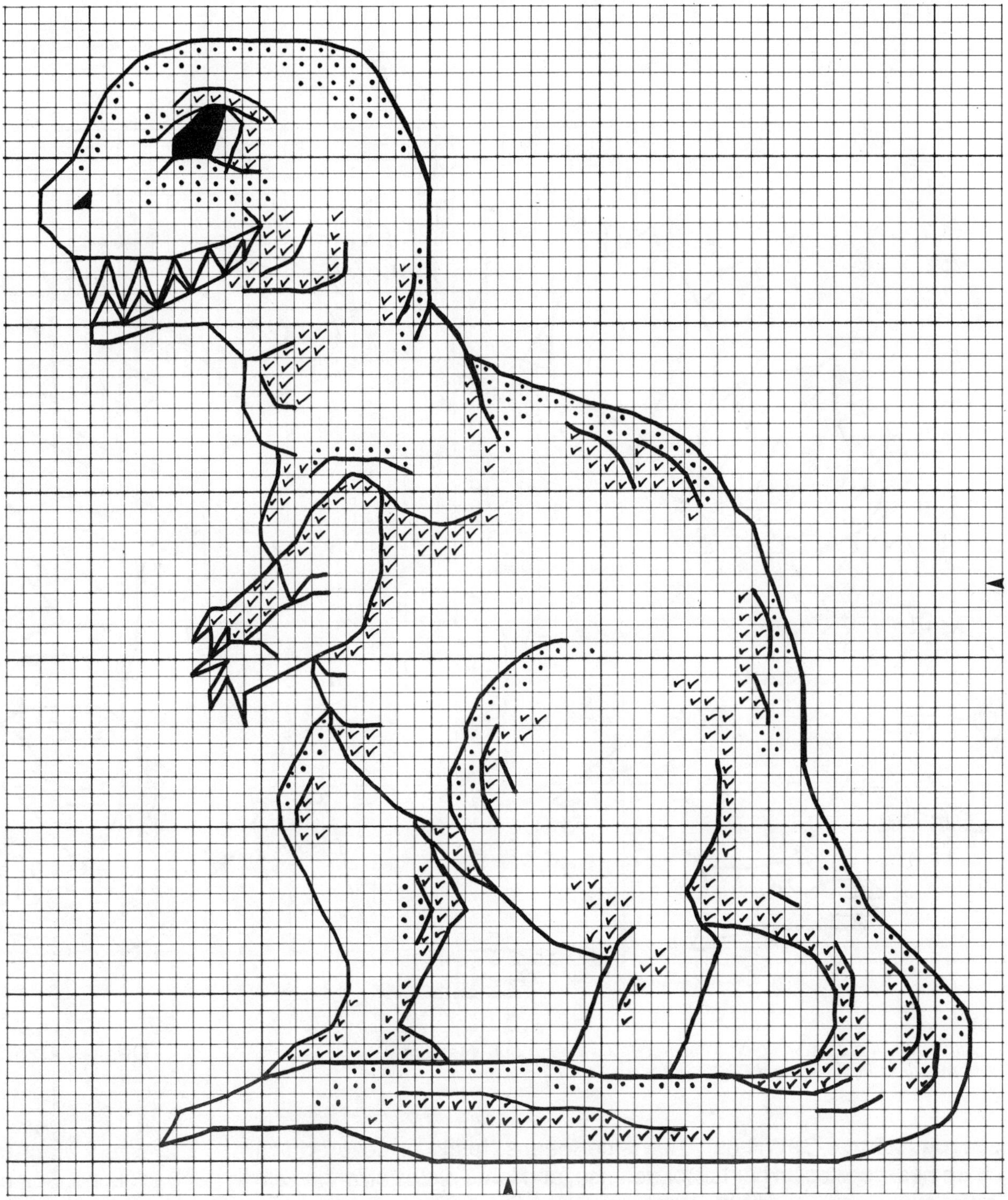

The model is stitched in the kelly green color combination on cream 14-count aida cloth. It is mounted in Wheatland Crafts' 5" x 6" Thin Line frame.

Design size: 55 x 67

Tyrannosaurus Rex (tie-ran-o-SAWR-us) The name means "tyrant lizard king." He was a meat eater with sharp teeth, some of which were over 7" long, which tore up the flesh without chewing. He stood on his two hind legs; his short forearms were hardly useful. He lived during the last era of the dinosaurs. His body was about 50 feet long, stood about 20 feet (two stories) tall, and weighed about 6-7 tons.

Stephanie Stegosaurus

The model is stitched in the salmon color combination on peach bud 14-count Aida cloth. It is mounted in Wheatland Crafts' 5" x 6" Thin Line frame.

Design size: 68 x 52

Stegosaurus (stegg-o-SAWR-us) The name means "plate or covered lizard." She was a plant eater with a sharp beak, spikes on her tail for defense, and large plates arranged along her back bone. Scientists wonder if she was either warm blooded or was the link between reptiles and mammals since the plates seem to be part of her circulatory system. She walked on four legs but might have been able to raise on her hind legs to eat from trees. She was about 30 feet long, almost 9 feet tall at her hips and weighed about 5 tons.

Trisha Triceratops

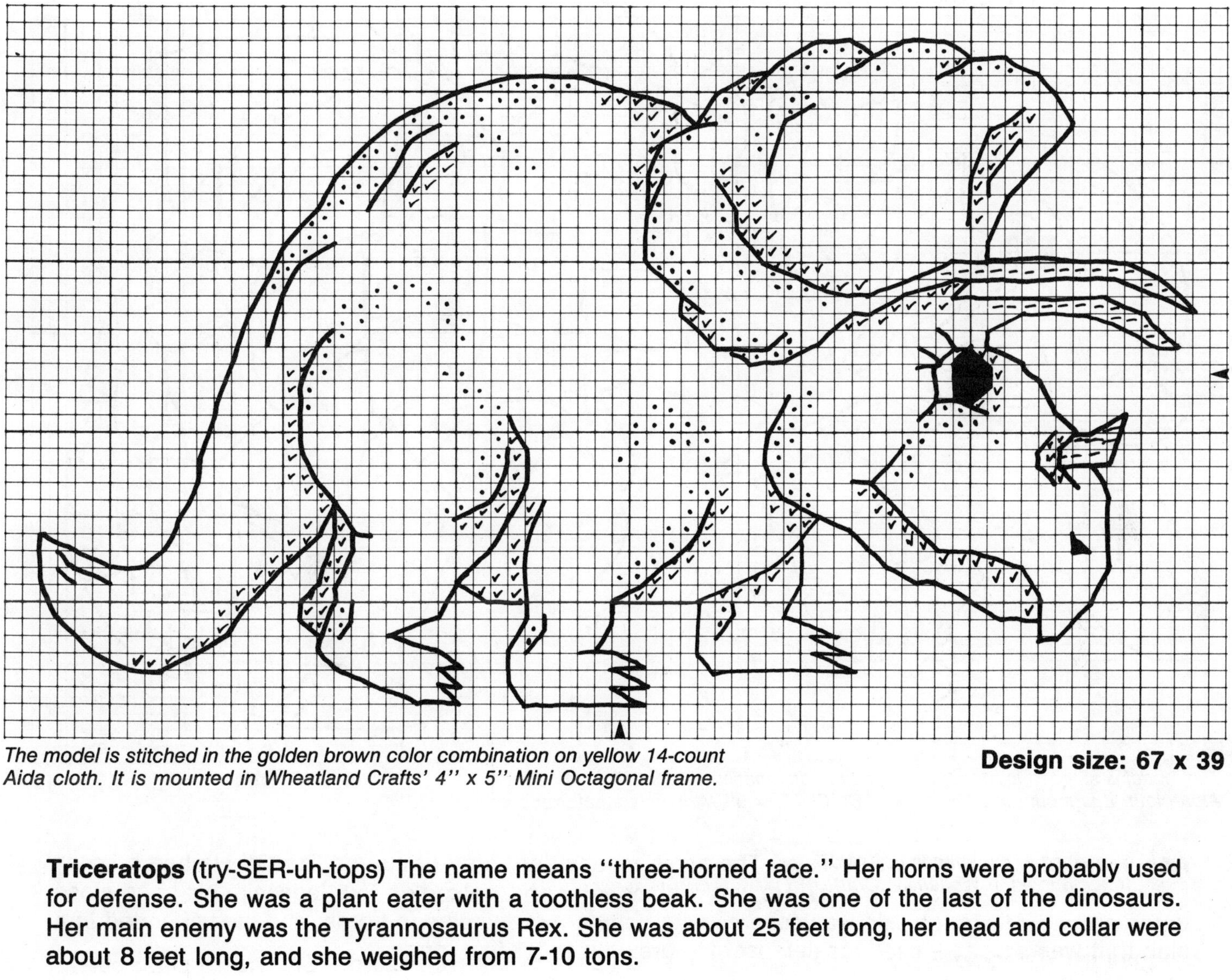

The model is stitched in the golden brown color combination on yellow 14-count Aida cloth. It is mounted in Wheatland Crafts' 4" x 5" Mini Octagonal frame.

Design size: 67 x 39

Triceratops (try-SER-uh-tops) The name means "three-horned face." Her horns were probably used for defense. She was a plant eater with a toothless beak. She was one of the last of the dinosaurs. Her main enemy was the Tyrannosaurus Rex. She was about 25 feet long, her head and collar were about 8 feet long, and she weighed from 7-10 tons.

Andrew Ankylosaurus

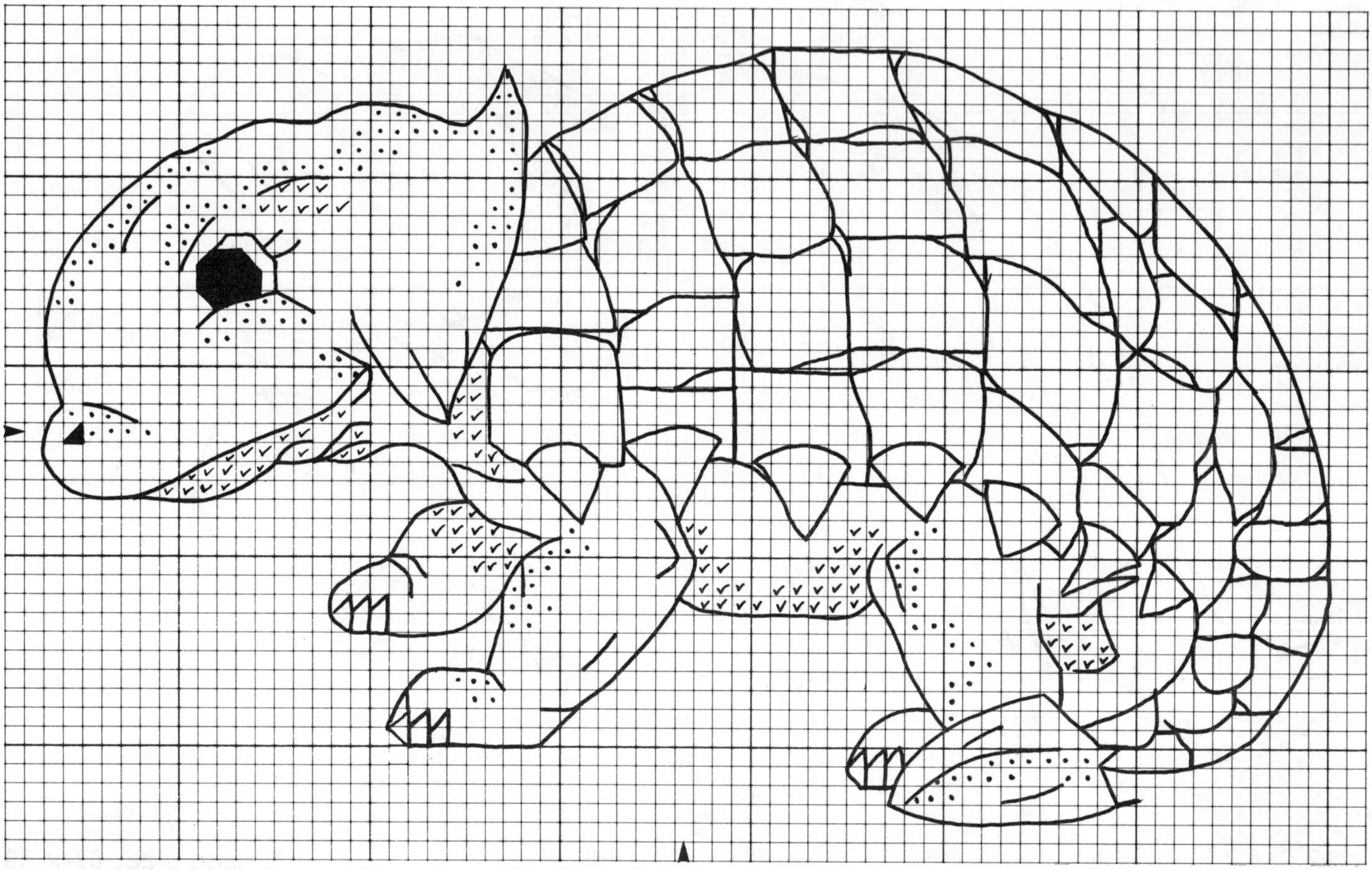

The model is stitched in the royal blue color combination on light blue 14-count Aida cloth. It is mounted in Wheatland Crafts' 4" x 5" Mini Octagonal frame.

Design size: 67 x 41

Ankylosaurus (an-KYLE-o-SAWR-us) The name means "armored or curved lizard." He had a horny beak, weak jaws, and a thick skull. He was a plant eater and walked on four legs with his head close to the ground. His tough skin was covered with bony armor plates and horns, and his tail ended in a club that was probably used for defense. He grew up to 35 feet long.

Peggy Plesiosaur

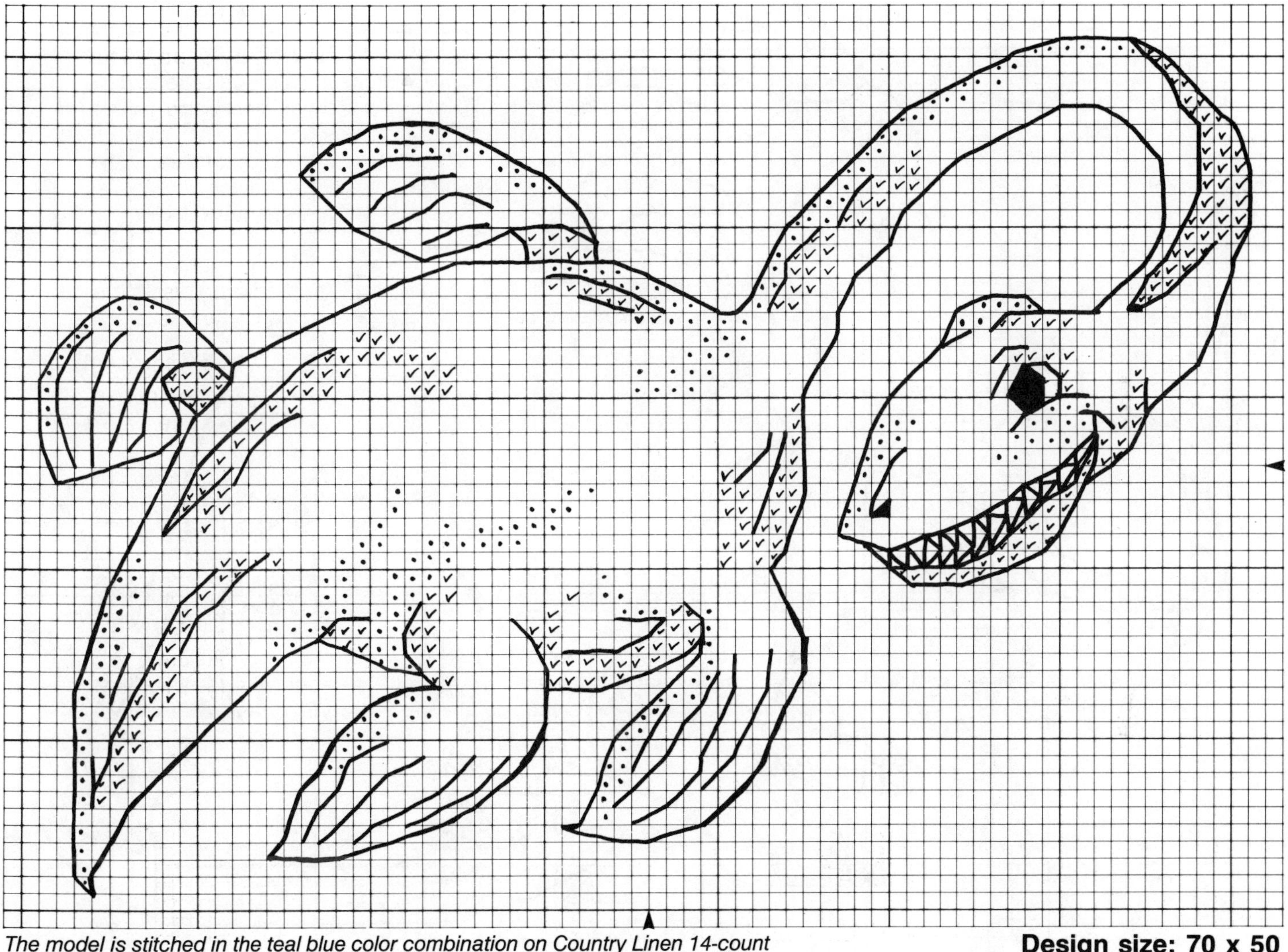

The model is stitched in the teal blue color combination on Country Linen 14-count Aida cloth. It is mounted in Wheatland Crafts' AC-111 big Stegosaurus frame.

Design size: 70 x 50

Plesiosaur (PLEES-i-o-sawr) The name means "near lizard." She lived in the water and ate fish. Although she had many sharp teeth, it is believed she swallowed her food whole because of grinding stones found with her skeleton. With a heavy oval body and flippers like a turtle, she was more than 39 feet long. Over half of that was neck and head.

Sylvester Styracosaurus

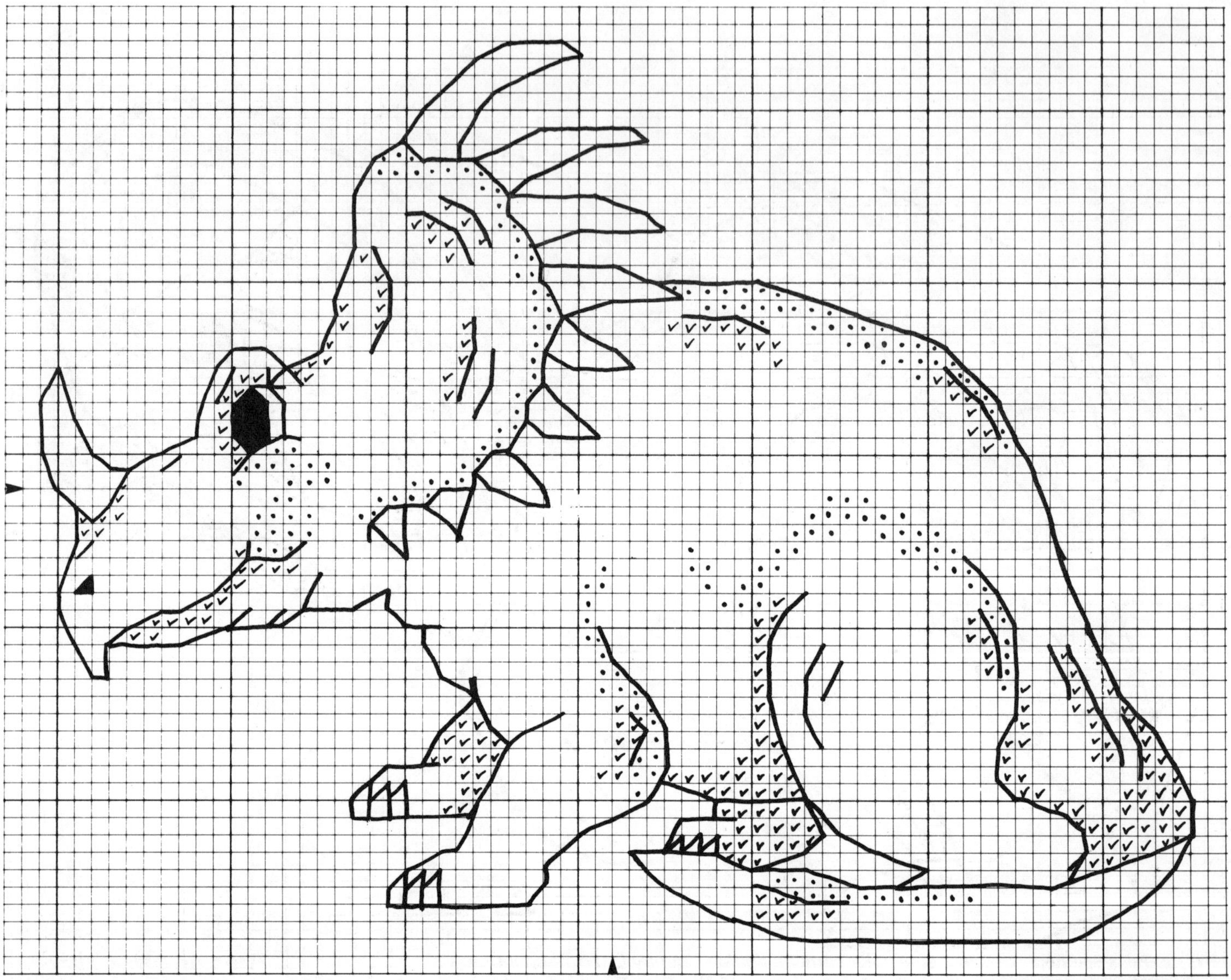

The model is stitched in the royal blue color combination on white 14-count Aida cloth. It is mounted in Wheatland Crafts' AC-113 Big Dinosaur frame.

Design size: 60 x 52

Styracosaurus (sty-RACK-o-SAWR-us) The name means "spiked lizard." He was a plant eater who walked on four feet. His most interesting feature was the bony frill behind his neck with sharp spikes or horns around the edges. He lived a very short time span in history. He grew to be 15-18 feet long and weighed about 3,000 pounds.

Peter Protoceratops

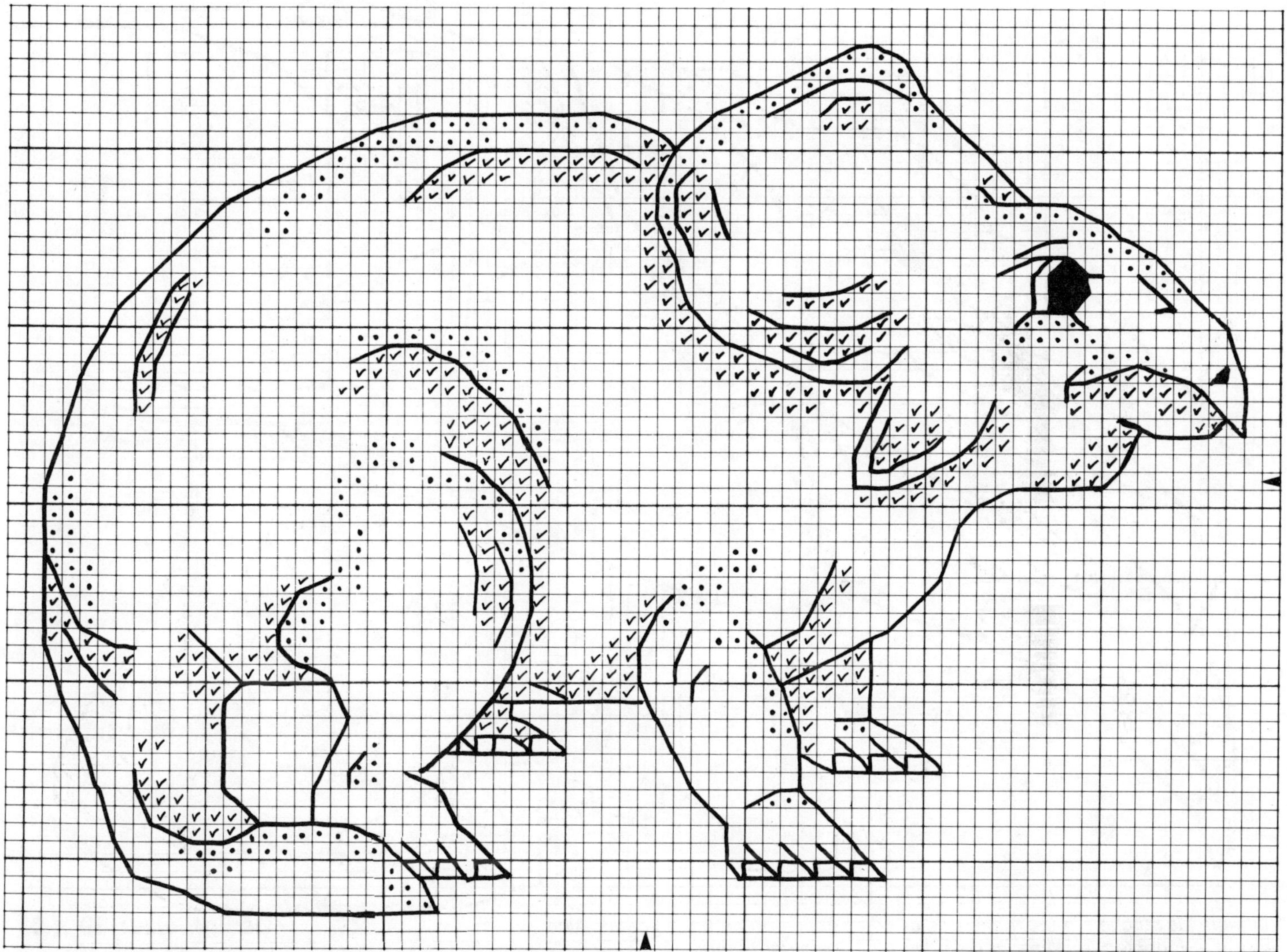

The model is stitched in the chocolate color combination on gold 14-count Aida cloth. It is mounted in Wheatland Crafts' 4" x 6" Thin Line frame.

Design size: 67 x 49

Protoceratops (pro-to-SER-uh-tops) The name means "first horned face." He is the best documented of all the dinosaurs because eggs with unborn babies in them, smaller protoceratops and adult sizes have all been found. He was a plant eater who walked on four feet. He had a sharp beak and bony collar with no horns or spikes. He grew to be about 5-6 feet long, was about 30" tall at his shoulders, but weighed about 3,000 pounds.

Penelope Pteranodon

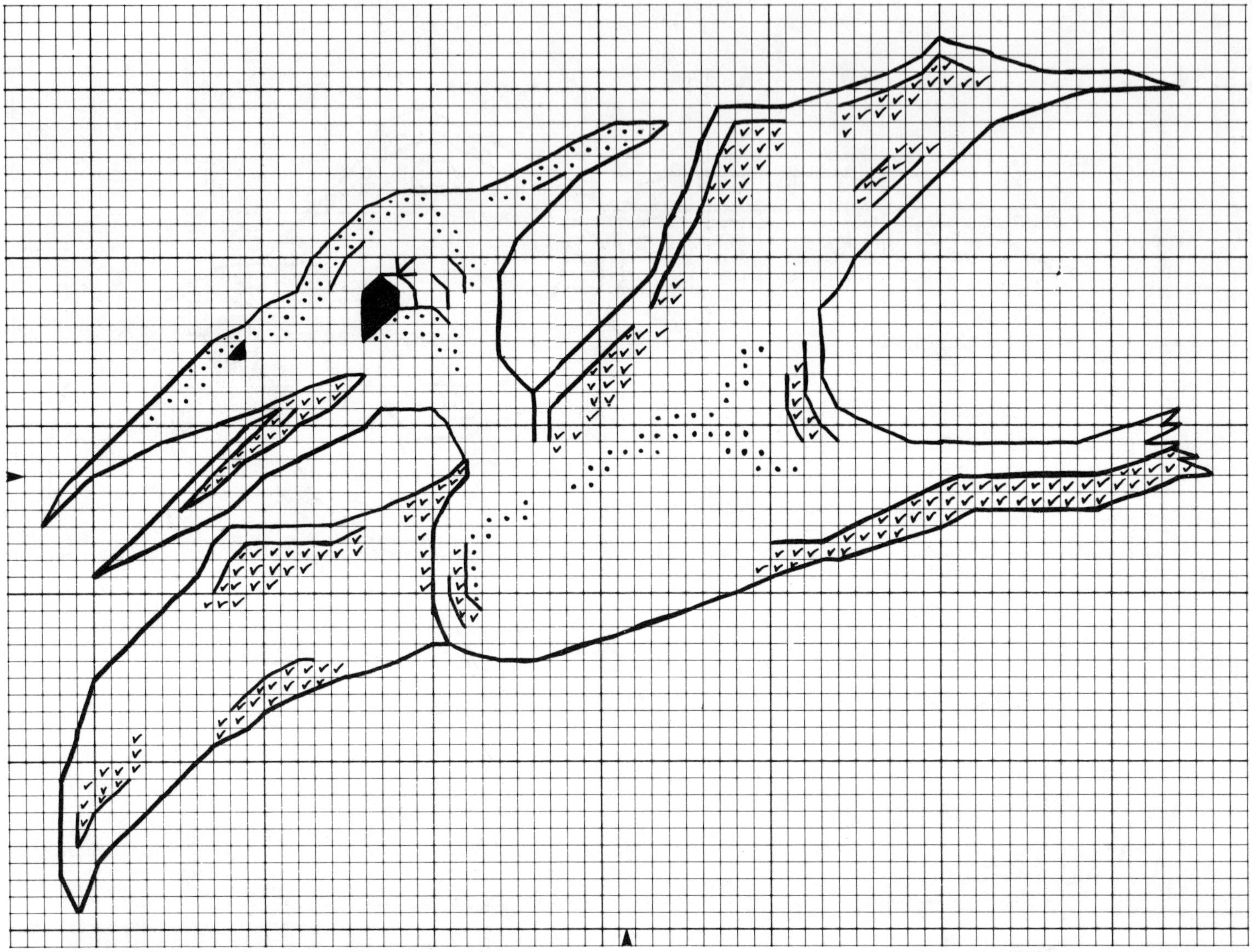

The model is stitched in the fuchsia color combination on cream 14-count Aida cloth. It is mounted in Wheatland Crafts' Mini Sunburst frame.

Design size: 69 x 52

Pteranodon (terr-AN-o-don) The name means "winged lizard." Her large wings could stretch about 20 feet across. Her small body, possibly covered with fur, was about the size of a turkey. Scientists believe that she could fly by taking off into the wind and gliding with the air currents. She probably caught her food, smaller bird-creatures and fishes, while flying. She had no teeth nor tail, although the crest on her head helped her flight direction. She weighed only 40 pounds.